Real Divas Win ™ Volume #3

REAL DIVAS WIN #3

"STORIES OF FAITH, SACRIFICE & VICTORY"

TIFFANY A GREEN-HOOD

REAL DIVAS WIN VOLUME #3
@Copyright (as collection) 2020 by Tiffany A. Green
All rights reserved. No part of this book maybe reproduced or transmitted in any form or by any means without prior written permission from the author.
ISBN: 978-1-953638-08-3
Printed in the United States of America

This book or parts thereof may not be reproduced in any form, stored in a retrieval system, or transmitted in any form by any means-electronic, mechanical, photocopy, recording, or otherwise-without prior written permission of the publisher, except as provided by United States of America copyright law.

**PUBLISHER
TA MEDIA & PRODUCTIONS LLC
DALLAS, TX 75240
www.PUBLISHYOURBOOKTODAY.INFO
WWW.TAMEDIACO.COM**

Unless otherwise noted, all Scripture quotations are taken from the Holy Bible, King James Version
(PUBLIC DOMAIN PER BIBLEGATEWAY.COM)

Holy Bible, New International Version®, NIV® Copyright ©1973, 1978, 1984, 2011 by Biblica, Inc.® Used by permission. All rights reserved worldwide.

The Holy Bible, English Standard Version. ESV® Text Edition: 2016. Copyright © 2001 by Crossway Bibles, a publishing ministry of Good News Publishers

Real Divas Win ™ Volume #3

DEDICATION

This book is dedicated to the many woman who have vowed to release their own stories to save thousands and millions of lives. This book was birthed not only to save lives but to also stand as an act of therapy and mental medicine. As we know, many women who experience the worst things in life are many times silenced and are threatened or too frightened to release what they've lived through. This then causes sickness, crucial mental illness, death and many other life issues that are untold. Women don't have to suffer; they can release through this platform and many others. The writers of the Real Divas Win Anthology are here for you and praying for your healing.

The sole mission of Real Divas Win is to comfort and allow a place for healing through writing to release, so that thousands of lives may be saved. It is our prayer that each and every word and chapter bless your life. May God Bless and Keep you.

TABLE OF CONTENTS

1 **YOLANDA IRVING**......8

2 **YVONNE HENDERSON**...........14

3 **STACY HARDIMAN**.........33

4 **JEANNINE M GAMBLES**.................52

5 **NICHOLE SHARPE**..................64

6 **JACCI SEASE**......................72

Real Divas Win ™ Volume #3

YOLANDA IRVING
MISTAKEN IDENTITY

One early Sunday morning, while I was at work, I received a text message from my mom. Now this is odd because my mother isn't a morning person, and she isn't that big of a texter either. So, I stepped away from the assembly line to see why she was calling so early. In a panic, she yelled through the phone and said, "Your baby has been shot!" I couldn't believe it. A million thoughts ran through my mind, I felt helpless, hurt and confused. In the midst of my chaotic thoughts, I gathered my things and made a mad dash for the exit door, I jumped in my car and drove as fast as I could to the hospital. Somehow as a mother, you think you protect your children always. So, I thought over and over, "How in the world could this happen?" With all the strength I had left, I ran to my baby girl. My heart was beating fast, tears were welling up in my eyes and just when I wanted to fall apart, God reminded me that He was in complete control. As I approached the ER, a million things ran through my mind. Would she survive? Who could do something so terrible? Would they find out who did it? Needless to say, I was a wreck. I had faith in God, but this was my baby, my daughter.

As I entered the hospital, the scenery made my heart sink. I couldn't believe that my precious daughter was lying in the hospital bed with a gunshot womb in her head and hand. She had been with other friends and it was a case of mistaken identity. They thought she was someone else and they tried to harm my daughter, but God had another plan. With her fast thinking she raised her hand to protect her head. The bullet went through her hand and penetrated her skull. As you can imagine, after hearing the doctor explain this miracle, I was overjoyed and angry at the same time. Overjoyed that

God had protected my daughter. Overjoyed that she was still alive. Overjoyed that she would live to tell the world about her miracle. Overjoyed that I get to hug her again and tell her how much I love her. I could not let my anger override the joy of the miracle. Just like any mother, I wanted justice and revenge for my daughter, but I remembered that the Word of God says, "Dear friends, never take revenge. Leave that to the righteous anger of God. For the Scriptures say, "I will take revenge; I will pay them back," says the LORD.' Romans 12:19. As my daughter began to recover, I realized that even during the most difficult times, God is with us; in fact, in those times He is carrying us. I know that the calm and nurturing spirit I had during my daughter's recovery was because I had confidence inGod; Blessed is the one who trusts in the LORD, whose confidence is in him. Jeremiah 17:7. As I put my confidence in God, I saw my daughter heal before my eyes. The hole in her head repaired itself and the hole in her hand recovered.

When I wanted to be mad at the person who had done this to my child, God reminded me that this was wasted energy. So, I took that energy and poured it into my family. My winning attitude helped me to build a lasting bond with my family and increased my faith in God. He kept my daughter and He reminded me that He has a plan for her life. When we as mothers win, our children win also. This incident caused me to reevaluate life in its totality. I am no longer interested in frivolous things. If it does not add value to my life, I'm not interested. My relationship with my children became better, because I am able to put first things first. As I looked back over this incident, I realized that I am a natural born winner. "But thanks be to God, who gives us the victory through our Lord Jesus Christ." 1 Corinthians 15:57 and because I am a winner, my children are winners too. This case of mistaken identity may have shaken my family, but it could not shake my faith!

http://bit.ly/YolandaCatriceboutique

YVONNE HENDERSON
ADDICTIONS

When you hear the word addiction, you think of drugs and alcohol. But an addiction is anything that holds you down, back or keeps you in bondage. An addiction is something you cannot go without. You find yourself thinking about it all the time. An addiction will make you do things you said you would never do. Even after you said you would not do it. An addiction will cause you to spend money on things you cannot afford. It will cause you to not pay your bills, take care of your family. An addiction will have you in places you never thought you would be or should be and will keep you there longer than you wanted to stay.

Addiction – The fact or condition of being addicted to a substance, thing, or activity. Addiction is a psychological and physical inability to stop consuming a chemical, drugs, activity, or substance, even though it is causing psychological and or physical harm to oneself.

After reading this definition you are probably picturing someone who is unstable, crazy, incapable of functioning in a regular or normal way according to society. If you think about it carefully, you know a lot of people who fit into this category of addiction. According to Hristina Nikolovska in his February 2020 article in Disturbmenot! more than 23 million individuals from age 12 and up suffer from a type of substance abuse disorder, in the United States. This is very alarming when you really think about it. This information lets us know; we know more people than we would probably like to admit who are struggling with some type of addiction. Addictions may not always be noticeable. Let me share just a few addictions you may be familiar with that I have met on this journey called life.

Looking at me or conversing with me you would never suspect I had an addiction. It is not something

I am proud of, but it is my reality, and it may be yours. You see addictions are far more dangerous than you know and has no respect of person.

The Smoker

One example is the person who has an addiction to smoking. It is not the act of smoking that brings them back, but the nicotine that serves as the drug of choice. Nicotine has an addicting agent that makes your body crave it. Nicotine curbs your appetite and causes you not to eat, well at least it did for me. Smoking was something I did out of habit for a long time. I had a cigarette for breakfast instead of food. There were times if I did not have time to smoke and eat at lunch time, I would rather smoke than eat. If I got upset; I needed a cigarette to calm me down. After sex I had to have a cigarette, I am sure most of you can relate to that. They did it in the movies and I thought it was cool. I started smoking at age 12 because I saw my older sister and her friends doing it. I did not have a job to buy cigarettes, so I would bum off someone else. My dad found out I was smoking and made me smoke almost a whole pack of cigarettes in front of him. Yeah, it made me sick and he told me if I wanted to smoke, I had to wait until I was 13, because that is how old he was when he started smoking. He also told me, if I was going to have a habit, I had to support it myself. I did not have a job, so I began stealing cigarettes and selling them to make money to buy more. My first business was stealing cigarettes and making a prophet from it. I found out I was good at selling things, so I began selling weed to my classmates. You see how an addiction can get you caught up in things you would never think would happen. Never in a million years did I think I would become a weed dealer in my town.

Years passed and I was still addicted to smoking. Then a turn of events happened, I got pregnant, I stopped smoking during pregnancy and as soon as I delivered, the first thing I wanted was a cigarette. I did not think it would hurt anything, but I was breast feeding. I got a chance to see firsthand the effects nicotine had on a person. My son became addicted to nicotine because it was in my breast milk. He became agitated, irritable, cranky, and fussy. I did not know it would have this effect on him. I took him to the doctor, and they told me he was fussy and cranky because of the effects the nicotine was having on him. I immediately quit smoking while breast feeding. I did not want to give up my addiction. When my son turned about 4 or 5, he did something that rocked my world. He called me one day from his dad's house and asked me what I was doing, I did not think anything of it, I told him I had just finished smoking a cigarette. He began to cry and asked me to quit because he did not want me to die. Even though I never smoked around him; he was still affected by my actions. He said smoking was bad and I needed to quit. After fifteen years of smoking I told him I would quit. I was good for about two years, then somethings devastating happened in my life that caused me to start back smoking to ease the pain and to ease my pain and quench my feelings of anger. At least that is what I told myself to be able to get through it. You see, when you go through things, that addiction is the first thing to come back. It stayed with me for another two years and I kicked the habit again for good. I can proudly say, that even when things got rough with the death of my parents, my mother-in-law and my sons father, I did not pick up a cigarette to make me feel better. I had the comfort of knowing Jesus Christ and through Him I could do all things with His strength, as stated in Philippians 4:16. One would think quitting for a loved one, especially a child, that would be enough, but what I found is that unless you give up an addiction for yourself you will never be free of it, it will continue to reappear.

The Worker

Another addiction is work. Yes, I said it, working too much creates a workaholic. I understand you must work to make ends meet, to put food on the table and clothes on everyone backs but working too hard can and will eventually pose a problem for the family. Like most baby bombers we said we did not want our children to struggle like we did. Well, as I look back, I wish I would have made my child want like I did. It did not kill me but it made me a hard-working person who would stop at nothing less than excellence. Kids nowadays do not have that same zeal; they feel entitled and things should be handed to them. I can admit, I worked so hard at times I only made it home to go to bed and then start all over again. Working is the most dangerous addiction, why do you say that? I am glad you asked. Working is controlled by society. Society puts a price on everything we need, then we must find a way to be able to purchase what we need. I guess one could say this is a direct result of the most important sin, which took place in the Garden of Eden. This caused separation between man and God the Father. As a result of their sin man was cursed to work the ground and labor for their food. If you do not believe me, look at your life. How many hours a day do you work? How many hours a week do you work? Do you leave work at work or do you bring it home? Do you give up your weekends to work? Do you give up time with your family to work? Do you take all the overtime you can get? If you answered yes to any of these questions, you are a workaholic. I can say this because I was one too.

I must say when I was younger, I did not find working hard to be a problem. Afterall, I started working when I was fourteen years old. I worked to be able to save. I hardly spent money, I just collected it and put it in the bank. That is probably why it is so easy for me to save now, because it was innate for me to do so. I had no family to worry about so, I worked. I wanted more than what I had, and I worked hard to get it.

I can remember paying my parents $200 a month for rent and paying a small bill every month. They taught me how to manage money, even though at the time, I thought it bogus that they were asking me to pay bills. Well, hell I was living there. I learned at an early age that nothing in life is free, not even staying with your parents. So, at the ripe old age of 21 I moved into my first one-bedroom apartment, where my rent was $525 a month. But because of what my parents did I was able to manage all of my bills and I vowed never to have to go back to my parent's house and I didn't until the marital separation. I was 6 months pregnant. That was the last time I would move back home. I worked so hard to make sure I never had to return to my parents' house that I lost sight of family. It was not until the summer of 2006 when my mom got sick that I realized I needed to slow down and spend more time with family. This particular year I decided not to work summer school for the first time and spend time with family, allowing my son time to spend with his grandparents, something I was not able to do growing up. In November of 2006, my mom passed away and in June of 2007 my dad passed. Not spending so much time working was one of the best decisions I ever made, however, it had its drawbacks. I found myself working more now that my parents were gone, and my son lived with his father. Working just seemed to be the right answer. It allowed me to forget about what was going on, but I never dealt with what had happened.

Fast Forward.

My son was practically raising himself. He had become a latchkey kid. I thought it would be different seeing I was a teacher and when he was home, I would be home, but it did not always work that way. I would work late to tutor kids. I became a sports coach and had practices and games all the time. The weekends were filled with church activities and left little time for home. After my ex-husband (my son's father) died, I worked even harder trying to make up for that loss. That did not work, the only thing I did was loss my son in the process. I was so accustomed to just buying him whatever he wanted to pacify him, I forgot to love him. I buried myself in work after his father died, not realizing he needed me, because he was hurting too. It was not until recently that I realized he was still hurting after 7 years; he had not dealt with the pain of losing his father. I made a vow to never again let work or ministry consume me to the point I did not have time for him. Even though I felt like I was doing good, I was hurting him. I came to realization that money was not everything and it could not solve everything. So, do not spend so much time at work or working to the point you neglect the ones you really love the most, and the ones who love you, your family. My son is all I have, and I had to learn how to balance work, home and ministry to make it a happy home.

Sex

I know, you were not expecting that one, right? Well, this was the hardest addiction I had to kick, why you ask? Because I did not want to admit I had a problem. Hell, if you asked the people, I was with it was not a problem. I was good at what I did, and I did not apologize for it. It did not matter if they were married, singled, male, female, acquaintance, stranger, long-term or one-night stand. After a while I became numb to it, it had no meaning I was like a junky needing a fix. I found myself in situations that I could not even explain how it happened. As I contemplated writing this chapter I had to go back and try and figure out how it all started.

What you are about to read may be a little graphic with explicit content.

    I can remember as a child playing with my cousins and one of my older cousins wanted to play a game where he was laying under the sheet and we had to climb through and get over him to get to the other side without getting stuck on the mountain. Well, I soon found out what the mountain was, it was his penis, on this go he stopped me and said I had reached the mountain top and it was my turn. I did not know what that meant until he pushed my head down and put his penis in my mouth and began to moan. I did not know what was going on, he eventually let me up and I went back and continued playing with my other cousins. Not sure what to do I never told anyone what happened. I did not even take a chance on asking to see if anyone else had done it, I just keep it to myself. The sad part is I remember the incident, but I could not tell you how old I was when this happened.

    Once I got older, I realized this was not a blood cousin, that was a relief, but it still was weird. That was my first sexual experience, and it was not something that I asked for or willing participated in. Although I did not lose my virginity until I was 22 years old, that first sexual experience set the tone for my sexual experiences. As an adult I found myself being curious about sex, but afraid to explore. In relationships I would go so far and pull back. I remember the fear I had about giving head to a guy because of that first experience. I will never forget the one time a guy held my head down so I could not get up, it frightened me because of the first experience, I did not realize he was enjoying it, I panicked and bit him so he would let me go and I got really mad at him, but I never told him why I was mad. I still had not dealt with the hurt. Every guy after that who would ask me to give them head, I refused, because it brought back painful memories. Memories I thought I had forgotten.

See the thing about sexual abuse as a child is that it sets the tone for the rest of your life and you do not even know it yet. As I grew up and began to have relationships, I could begin to see how that one incident had begun to shape my life. The relationships that I would have were not meaningful. I would be with men who just wanted to get off and leave. After a while I became numb to it all. Whenever I had sex I was not satisfied. Because I was never satisfied, I keep doing more and more to reach a level of satisfaction where I could stop, but it never stopped. Sometimes I felt I should be selling my services since I was doing so much, maybe that would satisfy me. Then I thought, I am not a prostitute, so I cannot sell my body. Hell, a prostitute probably would have thought I was crazy for doing it for free. Along with the sex I started to drink, I use to get so drunk and would fuck whomever I wanted. It did not matter if I knew them or not, if I set my mind to it, I was doing it. I had sex in cars, bathrooms, yards, alleys, I was so lost, but I thought I was doing what I wanted to. I had the mentality that if a man can do it, why can't I. I remember thinking men get praised for having so many sexual partners and are called "the man." So why is it when I have multiple partners, I am now a Ho (whore). I set out to change that double standard, so I got worse. I would have sex with a guy and never call him again, even if they called me. Very seldom did I have the same sex partner more than once. It had to be good for me to do that, but it had to be on my terms, because I could not have them thinking they were all that.

    Then the unthinkable happened, someone I knew, but was not sexually attracted to decide to rape me. I tried to tell someone, and they told me it was my fault because of my reputation. Just because I sleep with who I want, does not give anyone the right to violate me. Me the victim was being turned into the violator. I vowed never to tell again. I asked myself, so is this what would have happened if I had told all those years ago. Hell, I may as well keep it to myself and continue doing what I want. I am going to take out my anger on every man I meet. I would make them feel so good they would want to leave their wife and families, then I would stop. I had them eating out of my hands and other places if you know what I mean.

That got old and I started thinking about women, I never tried it until later in life, that was a whole nother experience, one I will never forget. I had been with so many men until a man could not satisfy me at all, so I said what do I have to lose. This experience most times was better than being with a man. I was in a dark place addicted to sex in any shape, form or fashion. With the woman I got into sex toys, I did not just use them with her I would use them when I was alone, because I needed a fix. I had to have that feeling all the time. I began watching porn to help me get off. I was watching porn on breaks at work and in the morning before I went to work, if I was not in a relationship, I would use porn and my sex toys to pleasure myself. This became a daily routine. It took a long time for me to beat this.

As I began to cry out to God for help, he began to reveal things to me that made since. He did not condemn me, he loved me unconditionally. He told me and showed me that I was loved by him. God showed me His love was deeper than any addiction I could have. I began to trust him and take Him at His ord. Understand now, I was saved. I had asked Christ to come into my life, so how was I having these problems. Christians do go through this; I am not supposed to be going through this. I learned that the sexual demons that were surrounding me were influencing me to masturbate, watch pornography, use sex toys and sleep around with woman and men.

Do not take this lightly, it took me awhile to get over these things and I still struggle with it, but I do not have to indulge in it. There are so many addictions, these are just the ones I had to deal with. I am not telling you this because I am proud of what I did, but because I am grateful for what God has done for me.

My Wins

God has taught me how to love my body and to know that my body is a living temple for Him. Knowing that helps me to keep my temple clean and free from anything that is going to tear down my temple. I love me now, so that way I can love others the way God loves. Love lifted me and it can lift you.

WWW.DRYVONNEHENDERSON.COM

STACY HARDIMAN
DROWNING IN UNFORGIVENESS

When it is said that death creeps in like a thief in the night it is true. No matter how prepared you think you are it sneaks up on your and snatches away the soul. Death comes in different forms and sucks the soul out of you. I was on my spiritual deathbed due to unforgiveness. I had the best-laid plans for my life, which were pretty cookie cutter. All I had to do was go to school, get a degree, get married and have babies, have a good group of friends, a good job, travel, etc. I did not think there was anything wrong with wanting that and I could not understand why my life's plan did not follow this path. What I failed to recognize is that I had a huge elephant in the room of my life…most of my life. That elephant was the spirit……..the heavy overwhelming spirit of unforgiveness. I did not realize this about myself and how this mindset of unforgiveness had blocked me from living my life fully. The unforgiveness was toward my mother; the vessel that God used to both birth and reject me. This spirit was rooted in me as a very young child, but I did not have language for things of this nature until I matured and grew into a person who understands themselves and those around them. As a child, unforgiveness rooted in me at the age of four. I lived with a great aunt and uncle for the first four years of my life and only saw my parents on the weekends. This arrangement was put in place to offset childcare expenses. My great aunt and uncle did not have children of their own and loved me very much and spoiled me as well. I was the apple of their eye. I have no recollection of splitting my time between my great aunt Mattie's home and my parents, so it was a shock to my system when I had to go live with them full-time. My great aunt and I would take daily trips to the corner store for treats and walk past a neighborhood firehouse where I would get more treats, smiles, and waves. Then one day we did not take our walk to the store and luckily the firemen thought to do a wellness check. My great aunt Mattie lay dying on the couch. She told me she was only taking a nap and I guess to not incite fear in me. The next thing I remember is my great uncle John rushing home and both of us jumping in the car and driving behind the ambulance with the siren blaring. I would not know it at the time, but my life would change forever. My parents rushed to the hospital and received the news of our loved one's untimely death and I never saw my Uncle John ever again. I now begin to live with my real parents, and we don't know each other at all. Unforgiveness started to set up shop in my life in a way I could not understand as a child and started my path to pain. Being uprooted, being parented differently, and now attending nursery school all day around people who did not know my trauma of losing my great aunt began to create a learning curve none of us knew we would not successfully master. One day my mother bought a new pair of sunglasses and I asked if I could play with the old pair and she says, yes. She then added, "Do not take them to school and play with them, do you understand?" She asked and I replied that I understood her rule. I do not remember if I did this immediately or how much time passed but I remember putting those sunglasses in my coat pocket for safekeeping. I honestly had no intention on disobeying my mother; I just wanted to carry them in my pocket. Unfortunately, due to my parent's work schedule, I would get picked up at closing time which was 6pm or a few minutes later. One day in my boredom of waiting for my parents a light bulb popped on in my head and I remembered I had a distraction in my pocket. I knew my mother said not to "play" with them at school and technically I was not going to play with them I just wanted to hold them. As soon as I pulled them out of my pocket the director of the nursery school saw them and knew they were adult glasses. She began to scold me for having them and promised to tell my mother. Now why she wanted to do something like that I do not know but she did, and my mother was angry. My mother was so angry in the car and I remember starting to explain that I had just taken them out of my pocket to hold and I would not have had to do that had her butt picked me up on time. Ok.... I did not say that last part but I wanted to so she silenced me and we rode all the way home quietly. We arrived home and it was as if I had swung on someone in the playground or something because she was very upset to think that I had disobeyed her. Even as a child I thought it is just sunglasses but to her my act of disobedience meant I would grow up to be a wild woman or something. She leaned into my face and we were nose to nose, which I was not accustomed to being treated, and she pointed her finger in my face scolding me yet again about these stupid sunglasses. She had invaded my personal space and I remember turning my head to avoid the discomfort of the situation and she cold slapped me across my face so hard my nose began to bleed. She and I both stood there in a shocked stare and she cleaned me up and asked me not to tell my father. I did not tell him at all because who knows if she drew blood over sunglasses, I did not know what this woman would do if I told this secret. I did not tell the secret but the root of unforgiveness dug deeper and I can tell you this incident of this stranger, although she was my mother, slapping me across the face and not having my great aunt to make things all better set the tone for our relationship for our lifetime.

Now that I am back living with my parents, my mother is sharing her home and husband with a daughter. It seems as if this was a huge adjustment because I was in a different environment. I was never a bad kid at all, but our relationship seemed to be built on my mother being a disciplinarian. The unforgiveness root is being dug deeper and deeper as the years go by. What I did not understand at the time was that her behavior toward me had nothing to do with me but it had everything to do with how she as a woman was evolving and began to take back her life as well as her own relationship with her own mother. She seemed unhappy all of the time and seemed to commit herself to being woman first and a mother second. As she began to work to create a life, she wanted to live I, somehow, ended up on the back burner and this left me a motherless child. She was in the home every day, came home from work every night, and may have even cooked dinner but she did not mother me. My dad was in the home and he began to assume more responsibility in the home as she began to rebel from her role as my mother. It was not that she was a bad person or a bad mother.... she just was not mine. We looked so alike at a time in our lives I wondered if she found it hard to like me because she did not like herself or the woman she had become. She wanted what we all want. A husband who takes care of us and is our partner in life. She found herself in a role of a wife with someone who was a great guy but was flawed and not very helpful around the house. As she shed her old self, I, as a little girl, was a constant reminder of who she did not want to be any longer. As early as my memory allows, I remember getting speeches about how I needed to be independent, I would have no friends, and that self-preservation was key. She had been so hurt in her life and marriage that she set the stage for isolation. It is not my personality, so I instantly rebuked that mindset and that caused more issues. She was rough on me and being taught life lessons is fine as long as they are balanced with love and relationship and that did not happen. Anything that my mother deemed as weak behavior, I was chastised. No crying, no speaking up for myself, yet again I was silenced. This friction dug unforgiveness even deeper and I began to go into a dark place. For example, I had a best friend who was a bit more independent than I was because I was sheltered. She had much older brothers who schooled her on life and their significant girlfriends always took her under their wings and helped raise her. She was a little younger than me and my mother thought I was weak for not having as much confidence in some things as my friend did. There was this time in my senior year in high school where I needed my hair done for one of my senior festivities and did not have the means to go to a beautician to get it done. I was pretty much a kitchen beautician for myself and did a pretty good job at washing, cutting, and curling my hair but I did not know how to perm my hair. I asked my best friend to do it for me because she had experience perming her own hair and someone taught her how to do it. So, she comes to my house to help me with my hair and my mother wanted to know why she was there. We both stood there looking confused because she had never needed a reason to visit before. I had asked my mother to do it and she told me no and that I needed to learn how to do it myself. I did not disagree, but this was a special occasion and I wanted it done right. I had no time for trial and error. When I told her, my best friend was there to help me with my hair she lost her cool. My mother went into a tirade about how weak I was and how much better than me my friend was and if she could do it and she was younger why couldn't I. We both stood there in silence and barely breathing afraid she would continue on with her rant. I was so angry and more importantly humiliated. Why could she not see that this was important to me? Why had she never stepped up to teach me versus chastising me for not knowing things? I just did not get it. So, I tried to perm my own hair and for starters I was so afraid of burning my hair out I did not leave it in long enough so essentially it was a fruitless effort. I was so upset. How could she think so little of me and scream it in front of others? Unforgiveness grew deeper. My dad tried to step in and teach me about certain things about womanhood. He also bought me shampoo after my mother told me I could not use her products. My dad bought me sanitary napkins because my mother would not, and I did not have a job and could not buy on my own. My father taught me how to cook and the list goes on a little further. He basically mothered me in many ways the best a man could, but I needed her. She just wouldn't do it. We had a disconnect. This challenged our relationship even more. I had no guidance to develop into a woman of purpose and there was no room to be me. This was a lifelong battle because my father was not a big help around the house, she blamed me countless times for not offering to help pick up the slack. As a result of this, I was hand mopping the floors, cleaning the kitchen, and other chores at the age of 5. Honestly, what kid "offers" to clean a home? I was not who she was mad at, but I was the receiver of the frustration.

As the years went by, things got tougher because she wanted me out of the house. I did all of the chores, never talked back, never fought back, and was extremely mild mannered but she still did not appear to like me or like me being there. How could this be? I am her daughter for God's sake! I was liked by many people, but my own mom did not. There was no pleasing her but, admittedly, by this time I was ready to go and filled with stubbornness and unforgiveness.

I moved through my life learning and growing but I always hit obstacles. I began to develop relationships with those who met my needs of acceptance and validation but did not meet the needs I possessed to progress positively in life. I played it safe by only dating men who chose me never considering what I wanted or needed. I allowed myself to befriend those who chose me also not realizing that some people chose you to for ill intent. A lot of my life's decisions also suffered due to the affect unforgiveness had on me. My relationship with others is not the only thing that began to suffer.

My entire life was affected by unforgiveness in a huge way because I made a lot of decisions based on my emotions, thoughts, behaviors, body, and spirit and not from a healthy place. Upon leaving an emotionally abusive relationship that broke my spirit and attacked my self-esteem, I needed my mother once again and once again she showed up in the same manner she always had. That was by criticizing me and refusing to help me transition from that relationship. When I reached out for help she rejected me and called me weak and unstable. I needed a place to live and she basically told me no. I could not wrap my head around this. She had even asked me if he had been abusing me. He wasn't physically abusing me so I told her, no. It wasn't until I began my healing process that I understood exactly what I experienced. I was so furious with her and so much so that I was ok never speaking to her again. Unforgiveness had taken me to a deeper place of darkness. I did not understand how a mother who understood relationships and questioned me about mine could turn her back on me…. her daughter. It just did not make sense to me. That is when I asked God thousands of questions with the main one being, WHY ME? Why did I have this cross to bear? Why was I expected to love and honor someone who did not appear to love and support me? I lived through years of family and friends and parents of friends asking why she treated me the way she did, and I had no answer and still don't. The only thing God told me is that my purpose or one of them is to exercise forgiveness and believe me He has given me a plethora of opportunities to exercise that muscle. It was difficult and exhausting, but I did it. I began to forgive folks without measure…everyone except my mother that is. That was the hardest to do because resentment had also taken up residence in my life and I just could not handle forgiving someone who was to love me unconditionally but there were a ton of darn conditions. With my first steps to forgiving overall, I noticed a positive upswing in my life, but something was still missing. Every time and I mean every-single-time I would go to God in prayer to forgive my mother something else would erupt in our relationship that would send me back to zero. Not to get churchy about this but I definitely had to consult

God on this because I could see this blocking my blessings in a way nothing else had. I was a good person, correction, I am a good person and I do not know why I had to endure this level of pain. It hurt to forgive someone who cared less about being forgiven. Someone who did not or could not acknowledge that they were able to be forgiven.

So, one day I got tired of giving my power over to unforgiveness. I decided I did not want to become what I hated and that is someone who could not acknowledge their role in a situation. I decided to look at things from both sides hoping that I could finally have inner peace. I sat quietly thinking what I could have done. Then I moved onto what I could have done differently, and I still came up with the same thing…NOTHING! I did nothing wrong. I was the child and was not the one who needed to actively make things right between us. But why did that self-validation still not bring me any peace. God told me that this was not about me and to dig deeper and I did. Once I began to shed my own pain I was able to see my mother's pain. I did not have joy in not having a good mother and daughter relationship and I had to imagine that my mother did not enjoy having a poor relationship with her daughter either. No one plans to live of life of pain. Instead of digging deeper into unforgiveness, I decided to dig deeper in understanding about who my mother was as a human being and not just my mother. I recognized that she had a poor relationship with her mother. I recognized that she struggled to maintain friendships. I recognized that she was in a marriage that did not make her happy and there was a possibility that she felt alone in her own life. All those pains can make any person, man or woman, husband or wife, miserable in their spirit and miserable in their dealings with others. She too is a good person that got tangled in the spirit of unforgiveness. I can see that now. I had a conversation with my mother about her childhood and relationship with her mother and pathology of the mother and daughter relationship blew me away even down to the face slap she received as a little girl and remembered at the age of 74. She recanted that memory without prompting and I was amazed at how alike our journeys were. I let her talk and only spoke to provoke thought and introspection for her. If I am healing, I want her healed too. With this new understanding, the only way I could mend our relationship is with dealing with her as a woman and not only my mother. I think I understand more about her than she understands about herself. It helps me to overlook the "mother" behavior or the lack thereof. I had to fix the wounds that I assumed and hoped that time would, but it did not. Once I began to actively forgive and understand others, including my mother, my life opened up. My mind opened up. My heart opened up. As I was witnessing myself emerge from that dark place I began to self-heal, operate in self-love, learn to love others and their humanness. I felt free from the heaviness of unforgiveness. The weight had been lifted. I started to make attempts to mend fences and build bridges where I had burned some of the path. Some reconnections were successful, and some were not. The truth of the matter is that I was supposed to separate from some individuals and remain that way in love. Learning that everyone has scars to heal and do so at different times.

Now I am committed to living my best life, which is so cliché, yet true. I live under the mantra of live and forgive the rest will take care of itself.

JEANINE M. GAMBLES
LIVING OFF THE PRAYERS OF MY GRANDMOTHER

I always knew I was "different" or "unique" and partly because I was told at a very young age that I wasn't going to be anything, or I wasn't going to amount to much. As a young child, I thought I was bad or that something was wrong with me. Part of me believed it and part of me, my soul, knew something different.

I was born in 1971, at the height of the Vietnam War. The only father I have ever known had been home for about five or six years. I arrived in the middle of December. I have been told that I was greeted with tons of stares and assumptions. My mother has been deceased since June of 1983, but my birth set forth a chain of events and revealed the troubles that were plaguing our home: Drugs, Alcohol, and extramarital affairs. My parents were carefree and loved to socialize and party. The late 60's and early 70's was a time for psychedelic drugs, wild parties and freedom from inhibitions. My entrance into the world was the answer to some of those assumptions, but making my debut, I was my mother's child and her cross to bear.

If someone told me that I wasn't prayed over immediately by my maternal grandmother, I'd have to tell them, that's a bold face lie. I know my maternal grandmother prayed for me and I know I am living off of those very same prayers today. Maybe my grandmother didn't know this at the time, I had only learned it myself in my adulthood---but she carried me through her female reproductive system. When she carried my mother in her womb, the ovary that would eventually lead to my conception, was there.

My grandmother and I had a very special relationship and she spoke to me in ways that only I knew was meant to serve as a purpose for my life. She instilled in me to be humble and to never allow my skin complexion to cause me to have a false sense of entitlement. One of the most important lessons of my life. She revealed to me the difference between light and darkness and though I would likely feel this strong pull spiritually, I had better be certain that I was on the right side. She denounced all types of witchcraft and anything not of God, the Supreme being and Healer. She had a very strong prayer life, and it has blessed and kept my mother's children as well as my aunts. We all honor her, her legacy and her tremendous power and strength. My grandmother passed away in 2011. Ase'.

I struggled with my mother's death the most. She left and I had many questions, but by 1983 she was in another abusive marriage and after giving birth to two more children, she died in a mental hospital, Kings County---beaten, left for dead, unconscious. Or so they said. At 11 you don't get to ask questions about things of that nature. I chased her memories for decades. I lived in her shadows in many ways, and imitated parts of her life just to feel connected to her. Until it was time to face my past and learn a truth that I could be proud to walk in.

By 2016, sometime around October, as I was earning my masters in Family Therapy, I had to complete my family tree. In Family Therapy, we call it a Genogram. The assignment asked us to go back at least three generations and look at patterns of mental and physical illness, and relationship patterns. I knew that I would have to finally face some ugly truths about whether if I was illegitimate or not. I had been treated differently as a child, called ugly names because of my skin complexion, and basically told that my life wasn't worth anything. Give up. I didn't stand a chance. This of course came mostly from outsiders close to the family, people who married into the family and sometimes from people in my family, who were privy to information, which led them to believe that they had the right to speak into existence what would become of me. I had a praying grandmother.

I waited as long as I could before calling my maternal grandfather. He was the only relative left that would tell me the truth. We were close. I spent a lot of time with him during my summer breaks as an educator and I knew that he wouldn't lie to memories from the past that perhaps he had and the rest of them had buried for good reason. I was hesitant because for some reason I didn't want to burden him with me and what I was dealing with. The uncertainty that I left unchecked for so many years. The question of who my biological father was often sat on the tip of my tongue when we watched baseball, in the tiny living room that he and my grandmother held countless get togethers in with neighbors, or was the grandchildren's makeshift sanctuary filled with dishes of candies, old magazines like Jet and Ebony and the countless photo albums that we looked through each time as though it was the first time seeing our mother and aunt in their youth. Or pictures of us at the various stages of life and the laughter that followed when the same funny pictured was revealed, "remember this one?"

My grandfather was 92 at the time--- with all of his mental faculties. He was sharp. I reached out despite my fear and reservations, but I did it via a telephone call. And as usual, he was happy to hear from me, "Jeannine---Hey, how you doing?"

"Hey Grandpa!---I'm well, how are you?" We exchanged pleasantries and I just dove right in. I was expecting a family secret about a secret lover. A family friend, or unrequited love.

What I got was my 92-year-old grandfather fighting back tears, as he told me that my mother was raped at a party one night at our family home on 778 Halsey Street in Brooklyn, New York. My stomach immediately convulsed into knots and I was physically ill. But I had more questions, like, for starters, what did you just say? Where was my father? Was it one man or multiple men? His voice shook and he halted my questions.

"Look, your mother came home and told us what happened---she didn't know who. But we loved you and we never treated you differently and that's that." And he was right. It was the paternal side that always had to knock me down a peg. Always reminding me that I wasn't shit and wasn't going to be shit. Ironically, I carry their last name. I inherited a legacy that I share with my siblings although I leave most to them and just pay my part in necessary fees.

And to be honest, my father never disowned me. He made sure I had his last name. He instilled in me pride and this message, "You can do anything you put your mind to." And, despite what other relatives said, I believed him, especially since my mom died so young.

But what makes my story so unique? How did I make it? What's the real message? Well, when people see you as illegitimate, they "allow" certain things to happen to you. Physical Abuse from a stepmother who apparently knew the true story. Sexual abuse by adults, male and female, who saw me as this tattered child that didn't belong. And the self-hatred that I secretly carried within me because I needed people to love me and treat me like everyone else. Most of my adult relationships were short lived, filled with alcohol so I could stomach the intimacy. I was literally bound up, and miserable all because I could not connect to the right words spoken over me. I only heard the hate filled messages playing over and over in my head as I fought for my education, obtaining my Bachelor's Degree leading the way for many of my other siblings, fighting for our Country In Fallujah, Iraq, and publishing and writing my own books. I was suicidal for a lot of my adulthood---but it actually started I when I was in the second grade.

The real triumphs came after that phone conversation in 2016. It's almost like, that revelation, set me totally and unequivocally free. All of my why's were answered. I began to research my family history. My complexion wasn't from my biological dad, but a recessive gene about four generations down and those individuals were mulatto, not white. I also began to understand why I was treated differently. One side of my family thought of me as different, part of a monster, although there is no research that supports that if a person is conceived by a rapist, they have rapist genes. Or that they will lack agency, free will, or a mind of their own. My grandmother knew different---she knew that the God of all would have the final say.

Finding out the truth, opened me up to this power that was lying dormant and slowly I began to come out from a very dark place. I had Post Traumatic Stress probably from conception and it was compounded from all of the abuse I endured then all of the abuse I witnessed my mother endure, and lastly from serving in Iraq, which is what led me to that class in 2016. I decided to study to become a family therapist after my own therapist helped me uncover what I had buried: my sexual abuse trauma.

Like many women, sexual abuse during childhood was an inescapable and tormenting past that had a lasting effect on my life. I was jaded during some periods of my life and almost despised all men, then as memories resurfaced, I began to question women and their motives and to this day, I do not date dominant women or controlling individuals who make me feel like I have no power in the relationship.

Even though I had already given up alcohol in disguise of fake intimacy, I took the time to learn about myself, preferences, my level of comfort and the power of the word, NO. No, I am not interested. No, she isn't my type. No, I don't sleep around. And be okay with my sexuality being more about being attracted to intelligence rather than physical attributes. In fact, learning that my father was a rapist, turned me fully away from objectifying a woman---I found myself becoming even more concerned with our value and power within society. How we are viewed, when we are left out, or excluded from the table and more importantly, intersectionality.

Black women, women of color, and the ongoing fight for our truths to be heard:

A white woman can lie, and it believed by millions and a black woman or a woman of color can tell the truth and not believed by one. This is my story this is my truth.

NICHOLE SHARPE
FROM BONDAGE TO FREEDOM

The year of 1998 brought about many changes in my life and my children's lives as well. We were all still transitioning from living in the house where we were quarantined to one room. There was a lot of work involved with my children because I had to break off the foolishness that they heard their Dad say and re-teach them. It was so hard at 1st because they went from seeing him off and on to inconsistency from him for the next twenty-three years! There were no words for having to be deprogrammed from the mode of Domestic Violence. I now had to rediscover who I was trying to be, only thing with that is I truly didn't know myself. I had never had a grasp on who I was as a young woman and then to have children, I sunk deeper into panic and anxiety attacks because I had been judged so harshly and dogged by the circle of folk that I knew…I had been publicly humiliated because I was connected to him. All the public sins were birthed in private, but nobody ever got in his chest about the things that had taken place. The only time anything was said the effect of what happened is when some of the men that happened to be in the parking lot had to physically come and stop him from trying to push me through the windshield of a church member's car! Everybody started saying well why you didn't say anything? Wait, hold up swole up, I kept trying to speak up and let someone know what was happening, I got the cricket sound and I suffered in silence. He had everybody thinking that I was psychotic, but it was really him though. The church knew what was happening because I used to get phone calls telling me that they saw him at some bar or this place and that place....funny thing is that nobody was calling me to pray or lift me up. When I come to church and walk into the bathroom and everybody and the bugs get quiet as church mice, that's a for real sign that they been talkin bout you...play with it! I had to walk into this same church where everybody knew me and be judged because I was a young, divorced mother with three children. I was judged for working outside the home. I was judged because I didn't always wear dresses or skirts because of the jobs I had. I was under fire and under a microscope but this drug-crazed, so smart he dumb and used his smart for evil husband was walking around like yeah I destroyed her and I don't really care about her or them children. Listen, I saw through all that acting and drama in the church, I started learning who I was. I learned that I was called to see, hear and prophesy at a young age and that the folks I was around was not even able to see me or catch me in the spirit-realm! God had called me to do his work in spite of the hell that I have been through and caught my entire life as I remember! Now, there were some folk that God allowed me to glean from and learn the ways of God from them: Mother Bay, Mother Mossie, Mother Susie, Mother Stanley, Gram Anna. I learned how to call on Jesus name. I learned how to moan so the devil don't never know what you saying.

I learned how to wait on the Lord to talk back to you and how he knew what all my tears meant when I cried. The resounding thing that I always remember is that I was told to stay with God, you hear me. I answered yes ma'am, I will. You see, the laughing and pointing and the waiting to see what bad thing was going happen to me next, that might take me out this world. It didn't touch the newfound relationship with God and strengthening my faith. I was able to put one foot in front of the other and while I was holding God's unchanging hand. I got up from the dark places of shame, guilt, self-hatred, self-destructive behavior and self-sabotage. Then, I gave up the fascination of suicide, severe depression, panic and anxiety for the life of a young mother with three children under 5. I went work and school full-time to support us. God's hand, the grace he has on my life and his mercy has kept me from the ledge where I was flirting with ending it all and jumping to end my death.

What did I want to do when I found myself and my life tore wide open at the frame from the bottom? How did I get to this point in my life? I thought I had got past this part of my life where there was so much carnage and damage! I didn't have any words to say that would make this stuff disappear! My journey in this path started a long time ago. The enemy decided to sift me as wheat (Luke 22:31 KJV) as a small girl. Hold yer mouth with yer hand, it will be bumpy like a jalopy ride! As a young girl, I didn't understand what it meant to be chosen and set apart. I didn't know what predestinated before the foundation of the world meant. I am telling my story to shed light on Child Molestation and Domestic Violence and to give real-life accounts of my experiences that have affected my life so deeply and almost stole my life! This is not a patty-cake story with pictures. I have come to expose the enemy's tricks and tactics to destroy someone's life. I have an earnest and sincere prayer that all who read this story will have more insight and be able to let go of the pain that may have gripped your life. I am a survivor and if this helps one person then it is to the enrichment of my life. Before you read this story, please understand that this information may not be your cup of tea. This is necessary to be completely healed in this area of my life. I came to share my testimony that the hand of God is real in my life. My destiny in His Kingdom is set and my blessings and promises for are mine alone. He chose me to be one of those that will empower, encourage, ignite and impact others to move past the trauma. Step out on faith as Peter did when he walked on water believing and focusing on Jesus. It is only when Peter looks to the left and the right that caused him to lose focus and he had to be rescued. Have you ever had to be rescued? I needed to be rescued and saved because I am a survivor and I wanted to let you know that you are one too! Yes, some bad things have happened, but it doesn't define you. There is love after trauma, there is a new life after trauma, and more. There is purpose and destiny for your life, you are so much more than the things that happened to you, Embrace what is new because when you do, you will know that if the Domestic Violence and Child Molestation didn't happen to me, I wouldn't have a story or a testimony or message of faith. I am now an author, advocate, motivational speaker and strategist that will always let others know that God saved my life!

Real Divas Win ™ Volume #3

JACCI SEASE
Race the Relay of Life

If you knew your end to the beginning, would you run to it or run away from it? Yes you, I am talking about your life? Often times I would ask that question until I realized that I am responsible for my life, I create the narrative. People talk as if we have no control, yet they are so wrong. We all have the power to create the life we want to live; it is our choice to make. This does not mean attacks will not come; those are things that come to deter us, throw us off track, give up, discourage us, but we must continue the race. People see obstacles as bricks to hold them down, but they are steps to help you climb higher. Those challenging times have built a lot of mental muscle. As the cliché goes, "what doesn't kill you, can only make you stronger ". We all can allow that to be true in our lives, it's all based on our perception and how we process things.

My children would say, "mom you're old, at 42, you should be through; so, why are you just getting started, you've lived all the life you have?" Oh, how those words echo within the empty halls of my soul. At some point I thought they were right, life is over for me, I am old. Then I asked myself the question, Should I be through? Have I run the course and finished my race? These are the questions I ask myself daily. I realized, as long as I still have breath in my body, I cannot give up. So, for me, the race is just beginning.

Being out of shape more than half of my life, running has never been my forte; strangest thing, I have been running all my life, the relay of life. I have been running from abandonment, hurt, shame, rejection, disappointments, failures, my past, and now I am running to my future. Who would have thought when I have lived more than half my life in the dark, that bam...one day a light would come on for me? There was no magic to it, I made the choice to flip the switch. All this time I have been sitting in darkness by choice. Now the race begins!

It all began in 1977, my mom was married with 3 children, I was the baby of the three. My mother conceived a child at sixteen and was forced to get married by her parents. Love had nothing to do with this, she was forced to be with a man she didn't love and barely knew. She did not know much about life but what she did know she implemented. Being a teen mother was hard, she faced many challenges and one of those challenges was called my daddy. Over the years my father was very abusive to my mother, but she felt she had no choice but to stick it out, where was she going at such a young with three kids?

Although I was young, I can still remember the nights my mother would work midnights and my dad would leave us home alone while he went out to party. The many days he would leave and not even prepare a proper supper, the many days of fighting and yelling, the dark nights where candles had to be lit because the power was out, or water being boiled on the stove for us to wash up because the water was cut off. Those were the easy times, I also recall the days where we hid in the closet because our mom was working and the loan sharks came looking for our dad and they kept ringing the door bell and knocking on the door, he was gone of course. Then you had the straw breaking day, when some men came to our home and threaten to kill us all if my mother did not come up with the money, he owed them. He, my dad that is, always managed to lay low and disappear from the house days at a time when people came looking for him. I would think, he does not give a damn about us. I guess they could have killed us and afterwards, he would have returned home and business as usual. He was a certified sucker, that's all I could think. We had some scary, rough moments, but we made it through them all.

The year 1984 is where it all began. I can remember it clear as today. I was 7 years old. It was the year Marvin Gaye died. I could remember my sister crying as if we lost an uncle, as the news flashed across the tube TV. It was the year she finally became fed up and conjured up enough courage and strength to leave and never look back. Maybe the death of Marvin Gaye helped her. Marvin died by the hands of his very own father because he was trying to intervene in an argument between both his parents. If my mother had continued with my father, there is a strong possibility that same narrative would have taken place in my family. Young, my brother did not like what we witnessed, but was not courageous enough to do anything…the older version of my brother would not have gone for it.

The departure was painful to us as kids, although we had witnessed all the horrible things, he took her through. That day she put a period where there had been a comma for so long changed a lot. We wanted our mother to be happy, with peace and safety, but we wanted our dad too. We didn't know that he was incapable of loving us because he didn't love himself, at the time all we knew was we wanted our mom and dad, much like "the Huxtable's".

Well, that didn't happen, my father left to never return. It was not because he did not want to, my mother was not having it any longer, she was done. When she divorced him, he divorced us all. That is where it all began. The thoughts were, If I was not good enough for my father, how can I be good enough for anyone else. This is how I became vulnerable to the lies told to me over the years and I believed them. From that, I developed low self-esteem, the feeling of worthlessness and shame.

During the time when my father left, all I could understand it to be was he left me, he abandoned me and he does not love me. The pain and disappointment that came from that abrupt exit in my life hurt deep to the core. It is a pain and unforgiveness that I've carried for 42 years. Those unresolved issues in my youth created a space for me later where I devalued myself and settled for people that did not respect or love me. The empty void was one of love, true love; but because I did not know my worth, I was with people that could never fill that void. They only respected the value of my own self-worth. At that time, I had no value, I did not love me, and they reciprocated just that. I always stayed in a place of wanting someone and maintaining the feeling of never being enough.

For many years that brokenness existed, until that day finally came. I began to self-reflect and upon my discovery I realized the issues I had were deep rooted. Abandonment and rejection were the roots to a self-destructing life. It is was birthed in my youth and became worse over time. That hurt I carried affected me in many ways. When I was 18, I allowed that hurt to translate into, you are not good enough and that resonated in so many ways in my life. I remember thinking, you cannot go to school and finish, you are not good enough to do that. I still made a strong attempt to start college but soon afterwards, I dropped out. As a man thinketh, so is he... those words could not have been more true. I gave up because the only thing that was important to me at that time was finding a man to love me. A man to replace that empty void I had from my father leaving me. I'd been longing for that void to be filled all throughout my youth, but the real chase for that empty desire began when I turned 18. I became legal and had no limits, so I thought. I began running and chasing as soon as I graduated. I moved away, thinking that was the answer. All I can say is during that time, I experienced a lot of pain.

Then I was 28, married with three children. Thinking that I found the man to fill that space, that hallow space that echoed deep within my soul. Sure, the marriage started off rocky and we married for other reasons beyond love. I wanted a family so bad that I had this belief for false hope that one day it would manifest into what I had been longing for. But until that happened, I told myself I will stay strong and endure because at least my kids would have their father, unlike myself. I later learned that was not the answer. Not only did I hurt myself, but I hurt my children in the process. Now I am on the path of helping them forgive and heal early. They cannot allow the pain to hinder their life too.

Although, I had a husband and 3 children, I was still empty and hurting more and more. Instead of getting the life I always wanted, I ended up marrying my father. No, it was not him literally, but they shared the same spirit in many aspects. The very spirit that hurt me, now as a grown woman, I was clinging to. Some people with call it a generation curse, others would call it a vicious cycle, however it all means the same. That void I referenced earlier was never fulfilled, I was still empty, hurting, and longing.

As time went along, I allowed myself to deal with abuse on so many levels because now I have 3 children and there is no hope. No one would want me with 3 children, and we would be a burden. These were lies I believed.

So, I ran and ran; trying to open new businesses, work different jobs, go back to school on several occasions, and more, yet I failed. I failed miserably at them all. Nothing seemed to fulfill me. I was always sad and searching, passing the baton through different stages of my life, yet coming up short every time. I was trying to place temporary bandages over wounds that needed to be healed permanently.

Then there was an ah hah moment!!!

One day, my prayers were answered, my eyes were opened to my past and that journey of hurt. It's like going through your nine months of pregnancy and that last month your stomach feels as if it can't be stretched any longer. You can't walk right because the baby is laying on your bladder, you feel stuffed all the time, your back is hurting, your hot all the time, and you can't sleep good because that stomach won't allow you to be great but delivery day comes. Before you can give birth to your blessing you have labor pains and you must put in some work to push.

The healing process is just that. As your eyes are opened to all of your past, you have to embrace hurts from things you remember and things that are brought to your remembrance. Because the pain of it caused you to suppress it to a place of nothingness, a place where you remembered no more. Well, when you ask Yahweh to come in and help, he does it all the way; so, everything is exposed, and you have become strong enough to deal with it. He will give you the mirror to it all. Not only do you learn of your past, you will see all your messed upness and you must learn to forgive and love that person you see. It is then when the healing can take place. True healing takes place through forgiveness first. You cannot forgive others if you will not forgive yourself. There is no healing absent of forgiveness.

Through my healing process, I faced my demons that I needed deliverance from. Many that were exposed to me, I did not even know existed because of suppressed memory and generation transfers. Some of those things were rejection, abandonment, loneliness, low self-esteem, molestation, rape, abuse, self-deception, sexual perversion, debt and more.

You must be truly ready when facing your past to receive your healing and full restoration. Not restoration to where you were before, but where Yahweh originally created. Once healed, you are finally in a place where you can live your proposed life you were created for.

So there I was, 42, divorced, sick in my body, homeless, no car, depleted bank accounts, and yet I'm the happiest I've ever been and feel the most successful in all the years of my life.

How is that so when everything around me seems as if it's crumbling? I have finally released the daunting shadows of my past, I am healed, my soul screams out.

Although, I am short in statue, I felt as tall as a giant in my soul. Perception is everything; blinded by the mask of my past, I allowed that to alter my life, but not forever. When I finally healed from my past, I was then able to see, my father leaving was the best thing for me. That was done for me, not to me. I blamed no one but myself, but the amazing thing is, I discovered the root to the madness.

You can think you're healed from a situation but if you don't identify the root cause of it all, you are only dealing with surface healing and it will always resurface again. It is not until it is plucked up by the roots where true healing can take place, to never surface again. That is the hard process, because you must put in work. You must be open and ready to see your truths, accept them, then grow from them. It takes honesty with yourself and courage to dig deep within.

Now that running from my past is no longer an issue, I still choose to run. I am running this relay of life; building a legacy to have a baton of success to pass along to the next generations and for generations to come. So, my kids said what again...42, be through.... no way, I am just getting started. I'm running this thing called life, full throttle, top speed ahead.

There are many of you that read this passage and can find themself in it. I'm hoping you're already healed or can find something within this to help aid in your process of healing, but know, as long as you have breath in your body, you have an opportunity to live. Run for your life because each day is never promised. Live each day as if those could be the last moments of your life. Laugh even when no one else is looking because that joy is satisfying to your own soul. Love because that's what we were mandated to do and it the best and most rewarding feeling ever.

If you run your best race in this relay of life, I'll partner with you and cheer you on, because you are amazing and you deserve to live your best life.

STAY TUNED FOR REAL DIVAS WIN #4 IN 2021

JOIN OUR EMAIL LIST AT

WWW.REALDIVASWIN.COM

TO JOIN OUR MOVEMENT

VISIT

WWW.REALDIVASWINANTHOLOGY.INFO